Mary Clemmer

Memorial Sketch of Elizabeth Emerson Atwater

Written for Her Friends

Mary Clemmer

Memorial Sketch of Elizabeth Emerson Atwater
Written for Her Friends

ISBN/EAN: 9783337143282

Printed in Europe, USA, Canada, Australia, Japan

Cover: Foto ©ninafisch / pixelio.de

More available books at **www.hansebooks.com**

OF

ELIZABETH EMERSON ATWATER

WRITTEN FOR HER FRIENDS.

BY MARY CLEMMER.

BUFFALO:
THE COURIER COMPANY, PRINTERS.
1879.

ℓ

Elizabeth Emerson Atwater.

———————·———————

BORN IN NORWICH, VT., AUGUST 8, 1812.

DIED IN BUFFALO, N. Y., APRIL 11, 1878.

MEMOIR.

CHAPTER I.

WHEN a woman endowed with mental gifts in any special direction passes away, it is considered the proper thing to tell her story, and to do reverence to her memory. But every little while we see a woman great in womanhood pass swiftly and silently out of her secluded sphere, and there seems to be no one to uplift the virtues which she exalted, or to tell the story of a life fit to be the inspiration of every life that comes after it. One reason for this is, that so much may be lived that never can be told. She lived, she loved, she served, she suffered, she died—that seems little to tell the eager denizens of the world, rushing in every direction to seize the prizes which the world hangs everywhere almost within reach of its own. I may be mistaken: I may have been unfortunately placed, but I seem to know many more women who are struggling after these prizes—the prizes of fashion, of society, of wealth, of power, of fame—than I know women simply great in those unconscious graces of the soul which bring womanhood nearest to the Divine Nature and closest to the human heart.

Such a woman was the one whose perfection of character and of life can be but faintly reflected on these pages. The exhalations of the finest natures are as subtle, as illusive as the perfume of flowers. They fill every day of a life with pervasive fragrance; but, when they have passed on and higher, who may catch and transfix forever in the amber of recorded fact that exquisite memory! It is most fitting that the name of such a woman should be perpetuated in a flower. ELIZABETH EMERSON ATWATER, not the mother of children who could rise up and call her blessed, was the discoverer of plants new to science. One of these, "in honor of its enthusiastic discoverer," was named by Dr. Carl Muller, the distinguished Bryologist of Germany, "Bryum Atwateriæ."

ELIZABETH EMERSON was born in Norwich, Vermont, August 8, 1812. She grew to the first consciousness of childhood in one of those homes of plenty and intelligence in which New England abounds. At six years of age, through the intercourse of their parents, she became acquainted with another little girl of her own years in the neighboring village of Strafford. The daughter of Judge Harris, a man of substance and repute, this little friend bore the name of Janette Harris. In addition to his magisterial duties, Judge Harris kept the village "store." Here, in an immense crate, which was a receptacle of all the "paper-rags" of the surrounding country, these two little maids

played and "rummaged," and found new "strips" of start-
ling cloth for their dolls' clothes. This was the beginning
of a friendship that lasted more than sixty years, and was
not dissolved even by death. Janette Harris of that long-
ago time still lives, honored and beloved by all who know
her, the widow of Hon. Portus Baxter, of Vermont, who
died in Washington, D. C., 1868.

To her devotion to the memory of her life-long friend,
the writer is indebted above all others for the material for
this sketch.

Janette Harris had a sister—only one—"Marcia," who, with
herself, lived to become a beauty and belle famous through
all their State. But before that day of enchantment came,
the two sisters, with little ELIZABETH EMERSON, started
forth—not to seek their fortune, but to go to school—to
boarding-school which, in 1828, was more of an event in a
girl's life than it can be in 1878.

To hear Mrs. Baxter tell of the journey to-day, is indeed
"a tale of ye olden time." Think of riding all the way
from Northern Vermont to Troy, New York, in a stage-
coach and that a sleigh! One gets a very vivid picture of
the three girls—the two beautiful blondes and the little
brune, ELIZABETH. The hoyden of the party whose pranks
filled the minds of her companions with dismay was Janette,
foredoomed, as a matter of course, by her vivacious tem-
perament to terrible home-sickness, when, for the first time
in her life, she should find herself far from father and mother
shut up in a very famous establishment for young ladies.
To educate young ladies seriously, elegantly and liberally

was at that day a far more exceptional process than it is at present when colleges and ologies for women are so diffusively multiplied. In 1828 the one famous school in the land for young women was Mrs. Emma Willard's Seminary at Troy. Here ELIZABETH EMERSON laid the foundation for that fine and careful culture which the leisure of her after-life as well as the proclivities of her mind made to her possible.

Yet, as we listen to the yellow, time-worn letters so sacredly preserved by Mrs. Baxter, we find that the school-girl of 1828 writes to her "Dearest Janette" wonderfully like the school-girl of 1878 writes to her "Darling Dovie." ELIZABETH EMERSON and Janette Harris happily went to school before the diminutive "*ie*" had robbed of their nobility three-fourths of the noblest names of womanhood. But in genuine girl fashion ELIZABETH EMERSON laments the departure of her mother to her "Dearest Janette."

TROY SEMINARY, *October 18, 1827.*

Mother left us before the stage passengers had breakfasted, and Abba and myself had to wait there all alone until they were to start, which was half an hour ; I suppose that time to you, Janette, seems very short, but to us, I assure you, it seemed a *long, long* time. Can you, my dearest Janette, imagine my feelings when the carriage came to the door? You may conceive in some measure that they cannot be described. I thought there never was so cruel a woman as mother.

To us who know the "Battle of Prague" only as a laughed-at tradition, her allusion to it here seems to come out of the far past.

9

TROY FEMALE SEMINARY, *January, 1828.*

Does your father **intend** purchasing a piano for you? The last music **lesson** I took, was a part of the "Battle of Prague."

I am housekeeper (no, not housekeeper—room-keeper) this week; have risen every morning before **six** o'clock and made a fire out of paper, lighted my lamp, and put my room in order before the "warning bell." Now, Janette, don't you think **I** am a smart child?

My lecture in chemistry, in which I am to expose myself in explaining at examination, is Fluorine; **I** do not like it much.

As we recall the advance **she made in the science after-** wards, which made her the honored **correspondent of some** of **the** most **distinguished** Botanists **of the world, her first allusion in her early girlhood to her favorite science is full** of interest:

TROY SEMINARY, *July 21, 1828.*

I fear, Janette, you will **be disappointed** in finding me with no addi- tional knowledge of Botany, as **I have** attended very little **to it** this term; **have** collected very few flowers, **as I think** I have **not** been to walk since **the** last of June, and shall **indeed be happy once more to** get home, where I can ramble as I like, **and without a teacher.**

In 1829 we find the young lady at home again, in Nor- wich, making to her beloved Janette, very free, vivacious comments on one of the characters of the region.

NORWICH, *Jan. 1829.*

Janette, **I must tell you** Mr. Rifford passed two days with us last week, and of all the disagreeable objects, I think he is one. He is from morn- ing till night talking of Marcia **Harris; thinks there never was such per-** fection—he thinks Janette **he should prefer for a wife.** While here, he was continually **calling** for tea, tea—" Mrs. Emerson, a little more of your good tea!"

In 1830 her father, Judge Emerson, moved to a new estate and into a new house, which he had built in Windsor, Vermont. In the same house and on the same estate, the present Minister to Russia, Hon. E. W. Stoughton, to-day finds his summer rest, and his fair summer home. There is not a more picturesque spot in all Vermont than this, in sight of Mount Ascutney, and in one of the most exquisite corners of the whole Connecticut Valley. From this enchanting place a venerable young lady of eighteen deplores to her old comrade, " Janette," the days of their youth, *i. e.*, when they were six years old and "rummaging" for doll rags.

WINDSOR, *April 12, 1830.*

I am glad you have determined upon passing this summer leisurely, or rather that you have not attached yourself to the duties of a school. I am in hopes to be at liberty in May, when I shall anticipate and hope to realize a visit from you. It seems an age since you and I have exchanged visits, as we used frequently to do. How many happy hours we have passed together! Could old times, or rather the days of our youth, be restored, I fancy we should be found working dresses for dolls, or rummaging over paper-rags in the store; but to recall scenes and pleasures past, no doubt in our happier days, is a melancholy thought, and as I was just inclining to be merry, I'll leave this subject.

Nine years later we find her in this same pleasant home writing to her friend of a recent recovery from a severe illness, under date of

WINDSOR, *March, 1839.*

That the ills of this life, though they may impair, do never destroy the health, is indisputably evidenced to me in the fact that I am still a "sojourner on earth." You will deem me quite wanting in the share of fortitude allowed to woman; I am ready to acknowledge that the "lot" which fell to me was considerably diminished in quantity. Considering my stature it was doubtless regarded sufficient. In my estimation the ills I have encountered seem quite disproportionate to the object. But spring has come! The harbinger of genial suns and early flowers that I love so well—sufficient, I trust, to arouse my dormant powers; to prove the brighter, that they've slept so long.

In July, of the same year, she was married to Mr. Samuel T. Atwater, of Buffalo, N. Y. She writes of her marriage to her friend " Janette," in a letter dated

WINDSOR, *July 18, 1839.*

In your letter you desire remembrances to Mr. Atwater, and say "if he loves you, I love him." Mr. A. is sorry that you speak with so little confidence of his affection, and begs me to tender you his kindest regards, and say that it does not admit of a doubt. We were married on Tuesday (July 16) morning, at nine o'clock, rather privately, but few friends invited. I knew it would be a mere matter of ceremony to extend an invitation to your family to be present, whom of all my friends, I should be most gratified to have recognized on this occasion. The wedding was private ; in the evening we received a small party of friends, and thus passed off our marriage-day. Don't fail to write me ere my departure, and allow me this first time to add my changed name, though with continued affection,

Yours truly,

ELIZABETH ATWATER.

With this letter we part with her maiden days. Serene, most fair, they lie far back, touched by the enchantment of the past. They can be but dimly reflected on these pages by one to whom the earth was then an unknown sphere. But those who follow these lines may see, by the works that do follow her, that the days of her life and the clear perfection of her character more than fulfilled all the promise of her auspicious youth.

CHAPTER II.

Her Happy Marriage—Removal to Buffalo—to Chicago—Active Life
There.

IN her marriage Mrs. ATWATER entered into that rare ideal
relation with another human being which is reserved for
the elect pairs of this world. More than thirty years of
daily intercourse failed to wear away the fineness of its
charm or the sweetness of its fellowship.

In a letter to "Janette," written in Buffalo, February 24,
1840, she gives a picture of New Year's Day in that city
near forty years ago. She writes:

As you anticipated, dear Janette, the Holidays passed merrily with us.
It is customary in Buffalo, as in all the New York cities, for the ladies to
"sit in state" on New Year's Day, from which custom we did not choose
to deviate. Accordingly we " sat up (or rather *stood*) for company " and
received seventy-six calls from the beaux of our city. We prepared a
table of refreshments, of which all made it a ceremony to partake—
though sparingly, as the same ceremony was observed in every successive
calling place. The wines and champagne were not wholly neglected.
The fluids seemed in greater requisition than the solids, though the sub-
stantials were occasionally partaken of, that the equilibrium be main-
tained. Those who paid their devoirs in the after part of the day
evidenced a little more *spirit* than those who called in the morning.
Yet none were so far regardless of the respect due to themselves and the
ladies whom they visited as to appear other than with propriety. It was
truly a merry season to all, and a novel one to me, for I have never

before chanced to be *deposited* where this custom prevailed Notwithstanding the hard times there are splendid parties at private houses,
assemblies, military balls, etc., constantly in agitation. My husband
and myself are so well satisfied with each other's society that we are not
necessitated to resort to such scenes for amusement or enjoyment, and
both entertaining the belief that there is no *comfort* in such scenes, no
good arising from a habitual attendance on them, we have refrained from
frequenting them, as many do—to dissipation.

The same year, speaking of the absence of Mr. Atwater,
on a business trip to New York, she says:

My husband found it necessary to go to New York on business, where
. he was detained nearly three weeks. He reached home Sunday last,
only to leave the following Wednesday, to return to-morrow. Now,
Janette, I can sympathize with you in the absence of your husband.
If ever I knew what it was to experience loneliness in a crowd it has
been in the absence of my husband. You will not laugh with incredulity
at the idea of my regretting an absence so temporary, for *you* have a
better self and can appreciate my feelings.

We have a regiment of officers stationed in our city, which contributes
much to its life. General Scott and his Aid gave us a call a week or
two since, when they were in the city. His Aid, Lieutenant Keyes,
married a particular friend of mine in Brooklyn, L. I. General Scott is
one of the most noble-looking men I ever saw, and vastly familiar and
agreeable in conversation.

In the winter of 1841, after speaking of the gaiety of the
city (Buffalo), she says:

Agreeable to Samuel T.'s and my own sage decision, such a disposition
of time is incomparably insignificant to the pleasures attendant on our
own domestic fireside, when, with books and work, and occasional conversation, time passes merrily, innocently and in realization of substan-
tial enjoyment. However, with an extended city acquaintance, it seems
a duty to occasionally receive and reciprocate such civilities. We regard

this interchange in the light of duty; for really it is at the sacrifice of every amiable feeling to make one's toilet at nine o'clock in the evening and proceed to a fashionable party.

The necessity of conforming to fashion, which is so fickle and arbitrary, is almost unbearable, and yet one cannot be independent of it, if they mingle in society at all; it is a sorry state of things.

In the two last quotations we find the key—the open sesame —to her entire nature. Small and slight though she looked, she was never lifted from her feet by any vanity of this world. Of an exquisitely-refined presence—with a person petite to daintiness, manners as delicate as they were winsome, radiating with the finest intelligence—she might have "shone" in what is called the most "brilliant" society, had "shining" been in any degree a purpose of her life. Born to the most refined and intelligent associations, she retained them to the last. But to be, rather than to seem anything, was so utterly the main-spring of her being that from very girlhood her character and life struck to the surest foundations. The purpose for personal improvement, which the average girl leaves behind with her school-books, was a prevailing impulse in Mrs. ATWATER to her latest earthly day. Nor in her did it ever degenerate into a selfish seeking after self-growth or mental perfection for her own laudation. She received to impart. She enriched science with the treasures of nature. With as hearty a largesse the gold of this world that came to her as her share she divided with the helpless and the afflicted. Never a self-seeker, even now it is easier to lay your hand upon what she did than to touch even by spirit that which was essentially *her*. The proofs of her exquisite taste, the results of her tireless industry, the monu-

ments of her endless benevolence remain. But even the
recorded words left to reflect her personal self are few and
far between. To those who knew and loved her, they are
the feeblest of pale shadows of her busy yet serene life—of
her symmetrical, subdued, yet strong and sunny character.
As the long years run on through her journals, reference to
her personal experience, to her personal emotions, became
less and less frequent till they cease almost entirely, and the
closely-written pages become compact records of the out-
goings and in-comings of her ever-busy, fruitful days. This
would have been a wise repression of herself had she been
possessed by an aggressive, egotistical self, which required
repression to keep it within due bounds. In her it was the
final and finest seal of self-forgetfulness, of pre-occupation
for others, of absorption in scientific and benevolent pursuits. The most noticeable fact on these pages is the frequent
recurrence of the name of every friend, even of those who
had passed but on the outer edge of her life. That these
journals to her were but mere records of reference was
proved when, before her death, she requested her husband to
destroy them all. Had imagination or emotion held her in
stronger thrall there would have been page after page of
glowing description, or of self-centered musing, out of which
might have been cut passages that to-day would have been
most precious to her friends. They would not have been expressed *her*, therefore we have them not. Hours that a more
subjective mind might have spent in thought, she spent in
active occupation. And the most certain expression of
ELIZABETH ATWATER's nature and mind we find not in the

pages of any journal whatever, but within the walls of Historical Rooms, and Museums of Science, and in the Home of the Aged in Chicago, which she aided in founding.

Of the happy years of her life spent in Buffalo we have no record outside of her letters.

In 1856 Mr. Atwater moved to Chicago. Here, perhaps, more than anywhere else, she sowed and reaped the richest harvests of her useful life. The writer must deplore that she herself holds no personal knowledge of those years. It seems indispensable to the perfect justice she would do to the memory of ELIZABETH ATWATER, that she should have had personal association with her during the epoch when her activity was greatest, her benevolence at high tide, and her ripe and perfectly-balanced powers at their prime. It hurts me to think how much more interesting and perfect this sketch would be could I tell all about the beginnings of that beneficent charity which she aided in organizing, and did so much to carry on—the OLD PEOPLE's HOME; and if I could but recall personally some of her acts of heavenly kindness to the dumb creatures of God in the HUMANE SOCIETY. This is not my high privilege. I can only reproduce the scanty pages on which her own delicate hand traced the story of one happy episode in her "Old Ladies' Home" life. Of a Christmas Celebration at the Home, she says:

Directly after dinner I drove down to the Old Ladies' Home, agreeable to previous arrangement; the weather being very severe, T. would not let me go in the cars. On my arrival found quite a number of friends of the Home and neighbors already assembled. A lady contributed two Christmas trees, one quite large and one small. I laid aside my bonnet and heavy blanket shawl, and went to work with the others

in marking gifts with the names of the old ladies who were to receive
them, and attaching them, or such as were not heavy, to the Christmas
trees. Handkerchiefs, skirts, shoes, collars, shawls, stockings, gloves,
nightcaps, alpaca aprons, calico aprons, Sontags, flannel, cotton, etc.,
etc., made up the donations to the old ladies. A beautiful writing-desk,
filled with all the necessary equipments, was our gift to the matron, also
handkerchiefs and a nice breakfast shawl from some other friend. The
old ladies had not the remotest idea what was going on down stairs, but
received instructions from the matron to present themselves in a body in
the parlor at the sound of the bell! Accordingly, when all the articles
were apportioned, and the empty boxes and waste papers and strings set
aside, the bell sounded, the doors were thrown open, and a procession of
eighteen old ladies descended the stairs and entered the parlor. And
now for the "ohs" and the "ahs," the interrogations (??) and exclama-
tions (!!) One said, "How could you keep this all so quiet? We thought
we were to have a very dull Christmas, nobody having called to see us."
After being permitted to walk around the trees and *see* the beautiful
things, they were requested to step into the dining-room and seat themselves, when they should be allowed to taste of *some*, and be presented
with others. Ice cream and several varieties of delicious cake were presented to each one in turn. I poured out the four pounds candy from
"*Gunther's*" on a huge platter, and passed it to one and all, saying that
each one might take as many as they could hold in one hand. It was
amusing to see the effort made to adapt the hand to the circumstances!
They all thought the candies were marvellously good. The ladies and
one gentleman present partook of ice cream and cake with the old ladies—
all but one. I improved this opportunity in going up stairs to visit two
sick ones who were unable to appear down stairs. I took a few articles
extra to these two, and to three more of my favorites who are invalids.
The dining-table looked very nicely, laden with ice cream and confection-
ery. The repast concluded, three ladies of us commenced to demolish the
fruit of the Christmas trees, by calling out "Collar for Mrs. Van Buren,
handkerchief for Mrs. Lavinea," etc., at the same time passing the
declared article along the *ranks* to the recipient. It was interesting to
witness the delight of these poor old creatures at being so kindly remem-
bered. All the old ladies kissed me over and over from very joy. They
hardly knew how to give expression to their gratitude. All being over,
I bundled up, bid adieu to all, and went home.

2

Again she writes:

This being our day of regular meeting, I visited all the old ladies in their rooms, giving poor old Mrs. Grant the snuff I purchased for her last evening. She was very grateful for my attention, and pronounced it the pure maccaboy—with a bean in the bargain! Old lady Horton was so grateful for the dress, that she had to give me an embrace with a kiss.

On her return from California, in September, 1873, she visits her old ladies:

I called upon all the old ladies, twenty-one in all. Gave them all shells and pebbles from "Pescadero." They were as much pleased as children.

CHAPTER III.

A NY one who recalls the reedy moors of Nantucket and its old quaint houses, will realize all that such a spot would be to a natural antiquarian like Mrs. ATWATER.

In 1858 she writes of it to Mrs. Baxter:

Two sheets of paper would not suffice to tell you of the wonders of Nantucket. The old, old dwellings with the horseshoe imbedded in the casing over the door for the purpose of keeping off the witches. This superstition I had read of, but doubted; now, my eyes have seen it. The old fire-places with tiles around them an hundred years old. These tiles represent Scripture scenes and some fancy pieces, and others Æsop's Fables. Some are red on white ground, some steel color, and some blue. There were usually from twenty-one to twenty-seven around the fire-places, according to the size of the chimney. We visited one house where the entire set was perfect. They represented Scripture scenes and were blue on white ground. Another, the residence of Capt. Albert Wood, had twenty-seven tiles around the fire-place. These were steel color and represented Æsop's Fables. It was too comical to see the wily old fox! I have always been crazy to have some tiles and am now rejoicing in some.

We visited the grave of John Gardner who came over in the "Mayflower," and went to see the first house erected in Nantucket which is still standing, built by John Gardner for his daughter's dowry. It has a horseshoe built in the front of the chimney.

One who remembers "the oldest house in Nantucket," standing as it does on the sea-washed moor aloof from the village, little and brown, and so old, stuffed with mediæval furniture on exhibition at ten cents per sight, will find it easy to "realize" the emotions of Mrs. ATWATER as she "revelled" under its roof. But Nantucket, rich in stories of the past and in trophies from every land under the sun, gave from its scarred old bosom to Mrs. ATWATER the one treasure that above all others could be dear in her sight—a flower. One sole flower, whose seed she believed was brought by birds from distant lands, for not the whole island nor America itself produced another plant. Of the precious "Erica" we will speak further on under Mrs. ATWATER's contributions to science.

Delicate, always hovering on the borders of invalidism, Mrs. ATWATER was not an extensive traveler, and while all lands contributed to her culture, she had never visited any shore beyond her own. But a long-anticipated delight was hers when, accompanied by her husband in April, 1873, she went to California. For years and years a supreme longing of her own and of her friend "Janette" had been to look upon the flowers of California. To the latter the first sight came a few years later, but in 1873 Mrs. ATWATER thus writes of them:

Oh the wealth of flowers! I could never have conceived such a paradise on earth. The thought of passing without plucking them compelled me to close my eyes and try and shut them out from my vision.

Again :

Took no dinner, but took the time when passengers were eating to secure lovely wild flowers on the plain beyond the track. At supper time repeated the performance. Some scarlet larkspurs I saw nearly distracted me ; I had never even heard of them before. On the bank of a river I discovered the beautiful flowering shrub that cousin Robert once had in his yard. I screamed on seeing it, and " T." voluntarily jumped out for it, recognizing it at once. This plant is worth the journey to the Redwoods, if we had no other pleasure. Oh the flowers! I could not step without crushing them. The most petite ; the most exquisite structures I ever beheld.

Mr. Blair had sent up to my room during the morning, a package of New Zealand ferns for my acceptance. There are twenty-four varieties elegantly prepared. He purchased the collection at Wellington, New Zealand. This is a most unexpected gift.

September 17, 1873, she writes in her diary :

Spent a morning finishing up the collection for Academy of Science, Buffalo.

Received a present from Mr. Bosi, of Florence, Italy, thus described : It is a magnificent work of art—the head of Mr. Lincoln, our late beloved president—done in Florentine mosaic. Underneath the head are represented delicate white flowers and rosebuds, copied from a little bouquet of pressed natural flowers which I sent to Mr. Bosi with a *carte de visite* of Mr. Lincoln, which Mrs. Lincoln gave me, saying, " it was the best likeness of him ever taken." The flowers were presented me at the old Lincoln home at Springfield, during Mr. Lincoln's presidency, by a lady temporarily occupying the premises. Thinking they might interest Mr. Bosi, I forwarded them to him with the picture, while we were boarders with Mrs. Lincoln and Taddy at the Clifton House. This exquisite mosaic is framed in an elegant bronze frame, and is altogether a gift to be coveted by royalty itself.

On the eighth of August, 1877, she writes in her diary:

Received newspaper from my friend Mercy B. Wright noticing a Grammar, which has recently come to light, written by my grandfather, Abel Curtis, when in college at Dartmouth. The book, which seems to be the only copy extant, is in possession of Rev. Henry A. Hazen, of Billerica, Mass. Have written a few lines to the owner regarding the book, and giving the reason of my especial interest in it that I am the granddaughter of Abel Curtis.

The thirteenth of August, 1877, she says:

Received response to my communication to Rev. Henry A. Hazen, relating to grandfather Curtis' Grammar. He is very enthusiastic over the discovery of this long-secreted book, and pronounces it almost beyond doubt the first English Grammar written in America. Says he shall take it to Bennington to exhibit at the Centennial next week, as beyond doubt Vermont's first contribution to the literature of the world.

CHAPTER IV.

I T is part of the irony of fate that many women especially endowed with the tenderness of motherhood should live and
die childless. This is so ordered that love which else might
be all lavished upon their own may flow forth through many
channels to enrich and gladden the world. Mrs. ATWATER
was one of these women. To hear her speak to a child or
to an animal, was to make you feel that you had never heard
them spoken to before. Says her friend Mrs. Baxter,
"There never was anything like her child-talk. Nothing
half so tender or bewitching." Children who would have
so filled and crowned her life were denied her. But because
of this she did not murmur or repine. She did not sink
down to idleness, fretfulness, satiety or selfishness. She did
not, as so many women have done, elevate her life solely to
housekeeping, to fashion, to society—or even to the Church.

Her tide of sympathy being deep, clear, still, could not be
absorbed by any one object, but, full of blessing, flowed out
over many. Literature, art, science, claimed her attention,
but more than all, benevolence! The religion of such a
spirit had nothing in it of the sounding brass or tinkling
cymbal. Rather, it suffered, and was always kind—how kind,

with that charity which is love, the unfortunate, the helpless, the dumb knew best.

One of the strongest passions of her nature was her sympathetic love for animals. Their silent life full of irresistible appeal went straight to her heart. Long before Bergh's name had ever been mentioned she constituted herself a "Humane Society" of one, and went into the most active operations. No one in Chicago was better acquainted with the *petite* figure, the gentle, deprecating face, the entreating voice of Mrs. ATWATER, than the drivers of drays, and the beaters of helpless animals. No street was too crowded, no crossing too dirty for those delicate feet to pass—if so doing she could reach the afflicted creature she essayed to help. No man was so rough or so cruel that she would refrain from uttering to him her spontaneous, tender appeal, to be merciful to the poor beast who at such terrible disadvantage shared with him the heavy burden of life. And few, indeed, were the men so lost to manly honor, or latent kindness of heart, as to listen unmoved to the entreaty of this gentle woman. They might resist the interference of any man; but a lady—"such a lady!" Oh! that was a different matter. Few were so lost to the possible sense of chivalry, but that they gladly withheld a few blows for the sake of rising a little in the estimation of "such a lady." The writer met, at the sea-side last summer, a lady from Chicago, who lived long in the same hotel with Mr. and Mrs. ATWATER, sitting at the same table with them. Still she said: "I never think of Mrs. ATWATER, but I see before me, as I saw more than once, that slender body leaning far out a high window, as she begged the man in the yard below to cease beating his horse."

When the Humane Society was organized in Chicago, she became one of its most active members, and in her journals we constantly meet passages concerning it. November, 1873, she writes:

I rushed over in a state of great excitement to see Mr. Sharp at the rooms of the Humane Society, and report a man who was cruelly beating a poor ox about his face and over his eyes.

During the prevalence of the epizootic, she writes:

Have grown so nervous from seeing so many poor sick animals compelled to do duty, that I could sit no longer at my window.

Again:

Horses are becoming more frequent on our streets, but I have not the heart to ride, even if they were going my route.

Was greatly excited at seeing a horse, one of a span attached to a large wagon, seized with apparent convulsions and falling to the earth. A great crowd assembled, and I was half frightened out of my senses, running down to the office of the Humane Society and requesting the agent to go and see about the matter.

Seeing the abuse inflicted on some poor oxen drawing bricks and stone, opposite my windows, I hastily laid aside my work, dressed in all the winter paraphernalia, and was just starting for the Humane Society, when Mrs. Shaw was announced, and after a call she accompanied me to the office, where I suggested to Mr. Bronson, the secretary, the propriety of watching these inhuman men.

The twenty-sixth of February, an intensely cold day, she writes:

The poor animals compelled to labor to-day must have suffered greatly.
Have been so annoyed at the inhuman treatment of a horse by a laborer, that I could not endure it any longer, but went over in all the mud
to State street, to enter a complaint to the Humane Society. The rooms
of that Society having been removed to Madison street, near the bridge,
a long way to go, in the mud, Mr. Sharp kindly said he would speak to
Mr. Brown, and have some person on the ground to-morrow morning.

Miss Stone called (October same year) weeping convulsively. She had
seen a splendid horse prostrate on the sidewalk, with his leg broken, suffering intense agony. Said he looked at her and groaned *so* piteously
that it almost broke her heart. I immediately accompanied her to the
office of the Humane Society and told Mr. Sharp of the circumstance.
He dispatched a message to the west side by telegraph to the surgeon in
their employ to come without delay, and sent a man to the protection of
the poor animal until further aid should arrive.

While at Pescadero, California, in 1873, she writes:

An old family dog accompanied us in our ramble. He is sick of con-
sumption, and very feeble, but inclined to go with us. He formerly
accompanied the family to the beach daily, and has rescued several
children from the sea. An immense Newfoundland, but his days of
usefulness are passed. He enjoyed the walk, but seemed very feeble.

Again, while at Stagg's Springs, California:

The old pet dog "Nigger" is one of the family here, and often follows
the guests on their excursions into the canons. He was savagely bitten
not long ago by several dogs. Mrs. Ware took all the care of him, and
washed the wound on his head daily, since which he manifests the most
intense attachment for her.

While *en route* to the Yosemite Valley:

We stopped at "Jerry Hodgden's," the regular stage-house, to rest a
moment, as well as to leave a little black dog that we found in the wilder-
ness, six miles back. He implored us, as plainly as a dog could speak, to
take him into our carriage. I, of course, interceded in his behalf, and he
was overjoyed to be riding with us. We passed but one habitable cottage,

and that of the rudest kind. We stopped the carriage before the door, and asked if they (three men) would not give the little dog a home. They replied, "Take him on to Hodgden's." So to Hodgden's we took him, and to our astonishment found he was their dog, quite a pet, his name "*Billy*." It seemed that he was greatly attached to one of the stage-drivers, and rides on the seat with him frequently, and follows him off by stealth, though the "Hodgdens" tie him up. I was greatly relieved to know he had a home, and we were the means of conducting him to it.

Of a friend's parrot she says :

Her parrot manifested the greatest pleasure at seeing me, leaving her perch immediately on my entrance, and sitting on my lap until my departure. Mrs. C. said it was an unusual manifestation of affection on her part; that she rarely condescended to such an extent.

With all her kindness, her extreme sympathy with animals, she was not one of those half-natures who allowed animals to supercede human beings in her affections or care. But when into the empty nest came little animals and birds, how much of the doting tenderness that would have been lavished upon a child was unconsciously bestowed upon them, we realize as we recall the story of the death of her little "Jo," a canary-bird, March, 1877. She writes of the death of little "Jo":

After dinner discovered dear little "Jo" lying in the bottom of his cage, apparently in great distress. Put him in my handkerchief and sat down with him near the fire. He soon had two spasms, and ceased to breathe. It has really made me sick to witness the little darling's sufferings. We have had him, and watched over him with the greatest solicitude, as we think, about twelve years—a gift from Mrs. Latham—a precious little treasure—I have cried myself sick. "T." feels his loss too. So fades away, one by one, the dear earthly attachments, wisely ordered, but painful to submit to. Have put him in a little tin box, with cotton and silk paper. " T." took the dear little remains over to " Katie's," to await the softening of the ground, that we may put him in his final resting-place.

Amid the delicate treasures long ago laid away by her tender little hands, I find an envelope, bearing on its outside, in her writing, the inscription, " Fidelity Dog," and inside the faithful record of this famous dog of Chicago, which I give:

The Dog " Fidelity."—This dog is an object of historical interest. On the night of the great fire, October 9, 1871, he took refuge in an open vault in the basement of the Fidelity Savings Bank and Safe Depository, 143 Randolph street, and remained there until the morning of the eleventh of October, when he was found unharmed. He is believed·to be the only creature that passed through the Great Fire alive. The event of yesterday was the appearance of that famous canine hero. the Fidelity dog. This grizzled and sturdy veteran is henceforth to be a permanent feature of the display. He will receive the visits of old and new friends at the stand of J. M. Terwilliger, the safe-man. The dog is the noble fellow whose memory is to be handed down to all fair posterity in connection with fire annals in Chicago. Pent up in the Fidelity vaults, he lived unscorched through those blazing hours when all the rest of Chicago toppled to fiery ruin. The fact that these vaults could perfectly protect animal life right through the fiercest conflagration ever known, was naturally accepted as permanent, irrefutable evidence of their invincibility to flame. Vaults and dog were henceforth famous—modern types of salamanders.

In the same case is another memento quite as characteristic of the woman who placed it there, three exquisite ferns issuing from one mossy root, folded away, their tissue wrapper bearing in Mrs. Atwater's hand this inscription :

Three sister ferns, Ellen, Sarah and Jennie, from west side of Pacific Lake, to which a new path has lately been opened, where were found these first beautiful mosses and ferns, August 16, 1877.

No added words can make more vivid the mingled delicacy and tenderness of so rare a nature.

In her journal we find these three personal records. Thursday, August 8, 1872 :

My sixtieth birthday! Who could believe it? And yet it seems forever since I went to Sabbath-school, and received the little blue tickets and red tickets in return for the verses from the New Testament which I recited. God has mercifully spared me these many, many years.

Thanksgiving Day, 1872, she writes :

It has not seemed much like the old-fashioned Thanksgivings of my dear mother's preparation. Those days are gone irrecoverably.

April 18, 1877, she says :

The grass is fresh and green, and spring indications are apparent. I long for the country. Are we mortals ever satisfied? A lovely mocking-bird across the street contributes greatly to my pleasure.

CHAPTER V.

WHEN ELIZABETH ATWATER entered the Troy Seminary, that institution was more in the land at that day than is Vassar or Smith College to the young women of our own epoch. The names of its principal and chief teacher—two sisters, Mrs. Emma Willard and Mrs. Almira Lincoln Phelps—will live in after generations with that of Mary Lyon, of South Hadley. Among the earliest and noblest pioneers of woman's advanced education in the United States, Emma Willard and Mary Lyon have passed on to the reward of their fruitful lives, honored already by the women of a second generation, who never looked upon their living faces. But Mrs. Almira Lincoln Phelps still remains upon the earth, in the full possession of her faculties, honored and revered in her venerable age. After fifty years have measured their cycle, she, at the age of eighty, lives to publish in the *Botanical Gazette* of September, 1878, her record of the *Bryum Atwateriæ*, discovered to science by ELIZABETH EMERSON, her pupil of 1828. She says in *Botanical Gazette :*

BRYUM ATWATERIÆ.—The discoverer of this plant was ELIZABETH EMERSON, of Vermont, a pupil at the Troy Seminary in 1828, when the writer (then Mrs. Lincoln) was preparing for publication her lectures on Botany. Some forty years after this, the former pupil visited the writer at her home in Baltimore, introducing her husband, S. T. Atwater, Esq., of Chicago. She had cultivated the love of science imbibed from her school-teachings. In affluent circumstances, without children, and with an indulgent husband who was happy to gratify her literary and scientific taste, she had traveled much and made extensive researches in Natural Science.

After the renewal of our acquaintance she was a faithful and attentive correspondent. At my suggestion she presented to the " Maryland Academy of Science" a valuable collection of four hundred botanical specimens. She was elected an honoray member of this society, which, after her death in Buffalo, N. Y., in April, 1878, paid a fitting tribute to her memory, as an earnest laborer in the cause of science.

We take from a Michigan paper an extract from an address of Prof. Albert D. Hager, before the Chicago Historical Society :

" Mrs. ATWATER was interested in several departments of science, but botany was her favorite study. During a sojourn in California she preserved more than two thousand specimens of plants, several of which were new to science." After recounting her valuable historical records, her philanthropic efforts, and her active and generous benevolence, the Professor closes by this remark : " It may, in truth, be said that the world is made the better as well as the wiser for her having lived in it."

The following extract from a letter of February 12, 1878, to the writer, gives the history of the discovery and naming of the *Bryum Atwateriæ :*

" I forward for your acceptance this little specimen. I believe you will feel an especial interest in it, from its having been found by your former pupil. I gathered it with other plants at the foot of the Yosemite Falls, in the Yosemite Valley, California, on June 24, 1873. It being an infertile specimen, I hesitated relative to pressing it, but was attracted by its peculiarity, and preserved several tufts of it. Attaching no particular value to it—being not in fruit—yet greatly interested in its appearance, I did not send it with other plants to friends for whom in my travels I am in the habit of collecting, but chanced to include one in a small parcel to my friend, Dr. Charles Mohr, a German gentleman, resident in Mobile, Alabama, and a fine botanist. He noticed it as new to himself, and immediately forwarded the tuft to Dr. Karl Muller, the distinguished Bryologist in Germany. I quote from Dr. Mohr's letter in reference to it : ' Dr. Muller describes that fine brown moss, of which you had sent me an infertile specimen, as a new species, naming it in honor of its enthusiastic discoverer, *Bryum Atwateria.* It is nearly allied to the *B. alpinum* of Europe.' It was reported in the ' Bulletin of the Torrey Botanical Club,' New York, August, 1874."

To this account of the discovery and naming of the plant under consideration, we will add that, though the name of the genus *Bryum* is ascribed to Linnæus, it seems to have been merged in with other genera of mosses, and is not found in the works of many of our distinguished American botanists. Lindley refers to Hooker for a description of the family *Bryaceæ*, of which *Bryum* may be considered a type. He enumerates more than a hundred genera of *Bryaceæ*, and says : " The little plants, the *Urn Mosses,* form one of the most interesting departments of Cryptogamous Botany ; they are distinctly separated from all the previous tribes by the peculiar structure of their reproductive organs." The position of the *Bryaceæ*, according to Lindley, is between *Jungermanniaceæ* and *Andræaceæ*. We have not seen what the distinguished Bryologist, Karl Muller, says of this peculiar family of plants. That he has honored our countrywoman in naming her as a discoverer, entitles him to our gratitude.

I will add to this article but one short sentence, worth more than all to her who is now in the better world—she was a Christian.—ALMIRA LINCOLN PHELPS, Baltimore, Md.

In Mrs. ATWATER's diary we find this allusion to Mrs. Phelps' acknowledgment of her discovery :

Received a letter from my old teacher, Mrs. Almira L. Phelps. She writes : " Mrs. Phelps rejoices over my discovery of the Erica, saying she is very proud that a pupil of hers, after forty years' separation from her, has discovered a new plant."

Earlier letters from Mrs. ATWATER to Mrs. Phelps refer to her contributions and relations to the Society of Natural Sciences of Maryland. Here is one written May 11, 1875:

DEAR MRS. PHELPS:

Through your instrumentality am I indebted to the "Maryland Academy of Sciences" for the honor conferred upon me of corresponding member. Complimentary as it is, were it courteous to decline its acceptance, I should have felt constrained to do so, not possessing the health adequate for the duties which a membership involves. I can but imperfectly maintain the extensive correspondence in which I have for many years been engaged.

The trifling assistance of occasional contributions of plants, culled in my travels in pursuit of health, I shall be happy to render. This will be a poor equivalent for the compliment offered. However, I shall throw all the odium of a failure in my duties upon shoulders too well known by the public to admit of a doubt regarding their capacity for the burden.

I regret not having visited the academy when last in Baltimore. I devoted an entire day to the wonderful collection at the Academy of Sciences in Philadelphia.

Before the Chicago conflagration of 1871, I was the possessor of one of the best individual collections in the whole Northwest—consisting of minerals, fossils, rare Italian marbles of exceeding beauty, precious stones, curiosities, etc., etc. All were absorbed in the devouring element, save a few boxes placed beyond the limit of the fire. My choicest specimens, at the solicitation of our lamented secretary, Dr. William Stimpson, were temporarily deposited at the "Chicago Academy of Sciences"—all were lost. I have had but little heart in the work since that terrible night. My herbariums were saved.

From Mrs. ATWATER to Mrs. Phelps, March 3, 1876:

I have felt great reluctance in forwarding plants to the "Maryland Academy of Sciences," knowing their facilities for collecting to be so great. However, have sent off by to-day's express a package of over four hundred specimens, and earnestly hope in the little collection there may be an occasional one of interest to the society.

3

Since I last wrote to you, added to the fearful effects of the fire, I received a fall in a peculiar way ; from the combined effects of which and the fire I abandoned the idea of delaying the plants for printed labels or a systematic arrangement. I have been particular in appending the localities and the dates, though in a very informal way.

I have for several years in my travels culled duplicates for the Buffalo Academy of Sciences—Judge Clinton, in response to my expressed hesitancy in sending common plants, emphatically saying *"send everything."* I consequently obeyed his injunctions, and *have* sent to him everything in my pathway. He is so enthusiastic on this subject that it has been a delight to me to please him. (He has encouraged this effort by occasionally praising me !)

I hope the plants will arrive in good order, and that, when they are properly mounted, you will have an opportunity of seeing the result of your pupil's efforts in wandering about our country. I send a fine specimen of the *Gymnogramme triangularis* of California, the lovely golden fern.

From Mrs. ATWATER to Mrs. Phelps, February 14, 1876:

This morning one of our managers of the "Old People's Home" called, leaving twenty tickets for me to dispose of in aid of an " exposition" at the Home for the benefit of our old ladies. I have been one of the managers of this, my favorite charity, many years. So you see I have few idle moments—not enough for my physical welfare. In a city like Chicago one can never fold their hands in idleness without violating the injunction to " love your neighbor as yourself."

Mrs. ATWATER writes :

BUFFALO, *Nov. 18, 1876.*
Saturday P. M.

MY DEAR FRIEND MRS. PHELPS:

I have treasured up, for a long time intending to forward to the Society of Natural Sciences at Baltimore, a specimen of the wonderful snow plant, *Sarcodes Sanguinea*, of Torrey. I send it first to you, for your inspection at your leisure at home. At any convenient time will you do me the kindness of forwarding it to the society. The society may be supplied with specimens of the plant; as they are not common, venture to send it. This was not of my own culling. I saw but one growing during my California explorations; that was inaccessible to me. The specimen I forward was plucked in the mining region near the " Calaveras Big Trees," about the first of June, 1871, by Mr. Stevens, of San Francisco. The plant is described as singularly beautiful. It grew near banks of snow three feet in thickness, at the edge of the snow bank where it was melting. The entire plant is of a brilliant ruby color, beautiful beyond expression.

The following is the acknowledgment of the receipt of Mrs. ATWATER's contribution :

BALTIMORE, *March 2, 1875.*

MRS. ALMIRA H. L. PHELPS :

It gives me great pleasure to be honored with the privilege of conveying to you the thanks of the Maryland Academy of Sciences for the gift of that interesting and valued specimen of *Bryum Atwaterii*. It was examined with much interest by many of the members present, and it would have been admired by a larger number on that occasion but for the particularly inclement weather of Monday evening. I return at the same time the letter of Mrs. ATWATER. Both letters were read before the meeting, and were the occasion of polite and grateful remarks by several of the gentlemen present. The specimen will be mounted on a sheet of our stout botanical paper, and will be carefully preserved as another mark of your kind interest in the welfare of the academy. Every moment of my time has been commanded by necessary duties, or I should have availed myself of your kind invitation to call upon you.

With highest respect and esteem, yours obediently,

P. R. UHLER,

President M. A. S.

Mrs. ATWATER for years was the correspondent of Prof. Gray, of Harvard College, whose works on botany take the precedence of all others in America. December 6, 1871, Mrs. ATWATER inclosed to Prof. Gray the beautiful stranger of a flower she discovered on Nantucket. The following is the copy of the letter, which since her death has been returned by Prof. Gray, for that purpose:

Dear Sir: In the summer of 1868, August 24 (I think), I discovered on Nantucket Island, growing wild on a sandy plain, the interesting plant "*Erica Cineria.*" On the day following this discovery I left the island, having no opportunity for making further search for duplicate plants, but suppose it must be obtainable in other localities on the island. Soon after my return I forwarded specimens of the plant to several of my correspondents—Hon. G. W. Clinton, of Buffalo, Prof. I. A. Lapham, of Milwaukee, and Charles H. Peck, Esq., State Botanist at Albany. At the solicitation of the latter, I forwarded to him a plant for Mr. Wood, who gave me in his last edition credit for the discovery. Meanwhile, several persons had written for specimens, and for an accurate description of the locality where found. The former I supplied until my stock *in hand* was nearly depleted; the latter I could not render intelligently, there being so few prominent landmarks to govern one; in fact, I was so absorbed in the plant that I was oblivious to all external objects outside the carriage until our drive was concluded. Since that time many persons have been disappointed in their investigations on the island, and I fear have questioned my veracity! I am most happy to say that last summer (1871) our niece (Mrs. Thomas E. Morris, of Saginaw, Michigan, who with my husband and a little niece were in the carriage when I first saw the plant) went again to Nantucket, with my strict injunctions to search the island perseveringly, and redeem my reputation, which I feared was occupying the minds of some indefatigable botanists unfavorably. She did so, and I have the pleasure of offering for your acceptance one of the plants plucked in the summer of 1871. Mrs. Morris thinks the specimens she has recently sent me were plucked, as she says, "from the same old roots;" and nowhere beside on the island could she find the plant.

And now, sir, I owe you an apology, not for proffering the plant (this I am emboldened to do by our mutual friend Mrs. Lewis), but for the informal preamble which I really felt to be your due. I have taken the liberty to inclose a Dianthus, which Prof. Peck thought had been previously found in the State of New York, and a pink Achillea from

Trenton Falls. If I can render you any service in the way of Western plants, I shall do so most cheerfully. I would gladly have sent you a more acceptable specimen of the Dianthus were it not that "since the fire" my plants have been inaccessible; this being the only one at my command.

Very respectfully yours,

MRS. SAM'L T. ATWATER.

Among the mass of historical matter contributed by Mrs. ATWATER to the Chicago Historical Society, was complete files of all the daily papers printed in Chicago from the tenth of October, 1871, for the following thirty days, which were the thirty days succeeding the great conflagration, in which $200,000,000 of property was destroyed October 9, 1871. Two trunks of "fire relics," picked up and purchased from different localities about the city, and each sample or relic duly labeled as to the places were found. Two hundred and fifty-three old and new almanacs from 1853 to 1878. One box containing all the daily papers printed in Chicago, giving a minute and full account of everything pertaining to the Great Sanitary Fair, held in Dearborn Park, Chicago, 1865, with a full account of what was exhibited, with badges and decorations, programmes, etc. Complete files of papers printed in all the cities through which President Lincoln's remains passed from Washington to Springfield, with all the proceedings at each place, and a full account of the assassination, with all the programmes, cards of admission to view the remains as lying in state at the Court House in Chicago, being a complete history of that event. A complete history of the great tunnel at Chicago, under Lake Michigan, two miles to the crib, from and by which the city of Chicago is supplied, with a diagram of the tunnel, crib, etc., published at the time of the inception and completion of the wonder of the day. A large amount of Confederate currency, and a framed picture of all the fractional currency of the Union government. Medals, too, probably 150 or more, some very beautiful in bronze, marking great events, and with printed scraps giving the history of each.

The following acknowledgment was sent to Mrs. Baxter at Washington:

CHICAGO, *Dec. 11, 1878.*

MRS. PORTUS BAXTER:

Dear Madam : I found your name so frequently associated with the valuable contributions made to this society by the late Mrs. E. E. ATWATER, that I wanted to see you and learn from you more of that excellent and remarkable woman, and with the hope that you might be in the city, in September last I wrote your son and expressed that wish. As I have learned your address by your esteemed favor of the 9th instant, I will take occasion to invite you to visit this Library at your convenience, and see the valuable contributions made by Mrs. A.

We have the coins, medals, metallic business cards, small paper currency or "shinplasters" and continental money arranged in a case by themselves, and as soon as we get the pamphlets, almanacs, autograph letters, etc., all bound, we shall have another case made expressly for the books, fire and war "relics," and other historical mementos, all of which will be properly designated "THE ATWATER COLLECTION."

On the eighteenth of last June, at a meeting of the Chicago Historical Society, a resolution was unanimously adopted expressing the thanks of the society for the interesting and valuable contributions of Mrs. ATWATER, a copy of which was spread upon the records of the society, and a notice of it communicated to Mr. Atwater. In addition to this, after enumerating the various articles presented, I read a brief biographical notice of Mrs. ATWATER, which was also spread upon our records, and subsequently published in the Chicago *Evening Journal,* a copy of which I sent to Mr. Atwater.

Agreeably to your suggestion, I send herewith a copy of the resolutions adopted by this society.

Very respectfully,

ALBERT D. HAGER,

Secretary and Librarian.

Resolved, That for the many valuable contributions made to this society by the late Mrs. E. E. ATWATER, we gratefully express our thanks, and direct the secretary to make a record of the same.

The above was unanimously and heartily adopted by the Chicago Historical Society, June 18, 1878.

A. D. HAGER, Secretary.

The following is the biographical sketch referred to by Prof. Hager:

GONE BUT NOT FORGOTTEN.

A TOUCHING TRIBUTE TO REAL WORTH—THE LATE MRS. S. T. ATWATER.

Many of our citizens who attended the fair given at the Jefferson Street Methodist Episcopal Church in February, 1876, will recollect the beautiful and rare collection of mosaics exhibited, and which were loaned for the occasion by Mrs. S. T. ATWATER, of Chicago. Mrs. ATWATER was a sister of Curtis Emerson of this city, was a lady of rare accomplishments, and was known to many of our citizens. She was an accomplished botanist, and corresponded with Profs. Gray, Clinton, etc., and she was also the discoverer of a new species of California plant, to which the scientists have given her name and credited to her in the later text-books. It will be recollected that Mrs. ATWATER died last April. In connection with the above the following extract from an address delivered before the Chicago Historical Society, by Prof. Albert D. Hager, Secretary, at the last meeting, will be of interest:

" Mrs. ELIZABETH (EMERSON) ATWATER, who for several years was a resident of this city and a patron of its charitable institutions, was born in Norwich, Vermont, August 8, 1812.

"She improved the excellent opportunities offered her for obtaining an education, and was a graduate of Mrs. Emma Willard's Seminary, Troy, New York. Upon the receipt of her diploma she did not quit her studies, but was an active student till the day of her death, which occurred in Buffalo, New York, April 11, 1878.

"Mrs. ATWATER was interested in several departments of science, but botany was her favorite study, her large herbarium gave evidence that she collected plants wherever she went. During a sojourn in California she collected, preserved and labeled, over two thousand specimens, several of which were new to science. In conchology, mineralogy and paleontology, she made large collections; these too were all carefully and accurately labeled. She did not make these collections for herself exclusively, but shared them with her scientific friends, and gave liberally to the Buffalo and Maryland academies of science, of which she was a member. At the time of her decease she had thirty boxes filled with botanical and other scientific specimens. These she requested her husband to give to the Chicago Academy of Sciences. He has faithfully complied with her request, and they are now safely deposited in that institution.

"It was not in the field of science alone that Mrs. ATWATER labored. The study of history and the preservation of historic facts also claimed her attention. She not only exhumed history from the records of the dead past, but caught it on the wing of the living present. In the same collection where she had packed two hundred and fifty-one old almanacs and other old documents marked "For the Historical Society," there were pamphlets and newspapers and hundreds of newspaper slips or clippings of modern date, each appropriately assorted and marked. In one package were slips referring to Abraham Lincoln and his peculiarities; in another to his assassination and the funeral obsequies that followed. Other packages were composed of slips referring to the war, to the great fire of 1871, to the rebuilding of Chicago, to the construction of its tunnels, to the sanitary fair of Chicago, the Home fair of Milwaukee; and accompanying these were specimens of the badges worn and numerous mementos from the battle-field, the great fire; and, indeed, the records of every historic event that has transpired during the last fifteen or twenty years has been carefully preserved by this industrious and thoughtful lady and generously given to this society. Were we writing a biographical memoir of Mrs. ATWATER *in extenso*, we would give in detail her efforts in organizing and sustaining the 'Old People's Home' and other charitable institutions of this city, and tell how earnestly she worked for the Humane Society, and cite instances of her active benevolence; but in this brief notice it must suffice to say that through her efforts science has been promoted, historic records have been secured and preserved, the aged and infirm have been provided for, the sorrowful have been made happy, and could the dumb animals speak they would bless her memory. It may in truth be said the world is made the better for her having lived in it."

Mrs. ATWATER bequeathed thirty boxes of valuable specimens to the Chicago Academy of Sciences, and the following resolution, in appreciation of the gift, was unanimously adopted by the members of that association :

WHEREAS, The late Mrs. ELIZABETH E. ATWATER, for several years an honored resident of this city, during her lifetime made a large, valuable and carefully-arranged collection of specimens of natural history, which she requested should be presented to this academy by her husband, Samuel T. Atwater, Esq., now of Buffalo, New York ; and,

WHEREAS, Mr. Atwater has faithfully complied with the wishes of his deceased wife, and forwarded some thirty boxes of specimens to this institution ; now, therefore,

Resolved, That for this munificent donation, and for the fidelity, promptness and care exercised by Mr. Atwater in carrying out the wishes of his deceased wife, the members of this academy hereby express their hearty thanks, and direct that a copy of this preamble and resolution be spread upon the records of the academy, and also that a copy of the same be sent to Mr. Atwater.

At the annual meeting of the managers of the "Old People's Home," held at Chicago, May, 1878, the following preamble and resolution was passed and entered upon record :

WHEREAS, Death has again taken one of our co-workers, Mrs. ELIZA-BETH E. ATWATER, be it

Resolved, That the managers of the " Old People's Home" have learned with sincere sorrow of the death of Mrs. ELIZABETH E. ATWATER, who died at Buffalo, New York, April 11, 1878, after a long and painful illness.

She had been connected with this society from its earliest organization in 1861, a period of seventeen years.

She was one of its most interested and active managers—faithful in the discharge of the duties devolved upon her. She won the love and esteem not only of her associates, but of the inmates of the Home, for whose welfare and happiness she constantly labored.

It is but a just tribute to the memory of the departed to say, that, in regretting her removal from our midst, we mourn for one who was every way worthy of our respect and love.

CHAPTER VI.

Last Days—Last Letters—Last Hours.

TO one who has loved to live, to whom life has come always full of blessing, the saddest days are the last spent in this wondrous world. Then the shadows deepen and close in upon the sight. Behind, the harvests are reaped and gathered. Before, no vast horizons open above the earth. The last dark river is reached. The startled spirit pauses on the brink, turns backward a gaze of unutterable love on the garnered treasures of a whole life—its work, its trophies, its friends, the best, the dearest, all to be left. With our best faith, what waits just the other side, who may know? Who can tell? But this we are sure of, that which we leave behind still holds our hearts with hooks of steel. Thus Mrs. ATWATER writes to her dearest friend "Janette," from Buffalo, January 30, 1878:

The parting-time must come to us all. But it is sad to leave this beautiful world so at variance with it as all this physical torture renders one. * * * * * * * * *
May God spare you yet a long time to your dear children and friends. I am willing and ready to obey His summons when it shall come ; still life is dear to me for the sake of loved friends. I have never been a society woman, my whole nature has revolted at it, but I have realized great enjoyment with Nature, with dear friends, and in my pursuits.

This is the last letter to her life-long friend. After more than sixty years of unwavering attachment, it was her tribute to the lovely human life she had lived, the life that she honored and loved, and for which she thanked God. Yet to those who know best the active benevolence of her life, its tenderness to the helpless, its care of the needy, its ceaseless charity, as diffusive and pervasive as it was widely intelligent; nothing in this summing up of her life is more remarkable or touching than its humility and utter lack of self-conscious assertion.

To her friend—herself that moment passing before the door of the Valley of Shadows—life looked different. Dear friends and dearer children were still left to her; but the dearest of all, the husband of her youth, had passed on before, and the bodies of four of her children rested within the circle of those far-away beloved Vermont hills. More beckoned her from the other side than staid behind to hold her here. The joy and loss of motherhood had never come to Mrs. ATWATER. She had many and dear friends. But the supreme pang of parting came to her when she looked upon the one she was to leave desolate. The dear comrade who, for so many faithful years, had been an unfailing staff to her tender feet, screening her from all the world's rude contacts; sheltering her that even the winds of heaven might not touch her gentle cheek too roughly; saving her from every earthly ill. He had saved her from everything hard to meet but the Angel of Death. When he came and would not be hindered, what desolation entered one soul—and it was not *hers!* To me there is something piteously touching in the last days

these two shared together on earth. As there must always
be something piteous in the final severance of any long,
sweet human relation.   It was born in spring—their love—
in the tender warmth of youth and hope; it grew the more
beautiful and strong in life's summer; but all the same came
the dreary winter of its rending—nor tears, nor prayers could
save it on the earth.   But as the earthly life recedes and
wanes the heavenly light shines more strongly and purely in.

As early as November 12, 1877, she writes in her journal:

I must now say adieu to our old pleasant home on Lake Michigan
shore.

In June, 1877, she had written to her friend of this home:

One look at the calm, green waters of Lake Michigan quells all
anxieties.

T. seems really happy to take the Evening Journal at the window, with
one eye on it and one on the lake.

At the final leaving of this beautiful home, in utter faith,
she writes:

God be praised through our Lord and Saviour Jesus Christ for all His
mercies vouchsafed to us, for all His forbearance with us. May He go with
us where we go, guide us by His counsel, and afterwards receive us and
all whom He has given us to love into glory.

Again, December 30, 1877:

The last Sabbath of the year! What a year of suffering I have experienced.   God has mercifully preserved us. May He continue to care
for us.

But as the pangs of physical suffering increased and the inevitable end drew near, there was no outcry, no murmur, only a gentle putting of the dissolving house in order, that when its final dissolution came there could be no unavailing regret. Not an object in her possession that did not have its place and final destination placed upon record. Not only had thousands of plants and specimens been classified and labeled by her delicate hands with laborious care, but not a friend or acquaintance in her last suffering days was forgotten. It was at this time that a little package arrived from her to the writer which called forth the following letter. At that time a prisoner in my room, from the effects of an accident, a disabled hand traced the letter without delay, so fearful was I that Mrs. ATWATER might pass where no letter could reach her before it could arrive in Buffalo, and so desirous was I that before she left the earth she should know from myself what she was to me as a woman. As my one last personal tribute to her in life I here record it:

DEAR MRS. ATWATER:

A little more than a week ago, as I sat by my window one morning I saw an express wagon stop; and, as my brother often sends packages to my mother, the thought never occurred to me that anything had arrived for me. Imagine my surprise and delight a very few moments later when I opened the pretty box and discovered within it another *prettier box.* It was more than kind of you, dear Mrs. ATWATER, to send this to me. I shall keep it for the sake of the giver as long as I live. I have nothing at all like it. I am glad of that. It is an exquisite little thing, like its giver, and I shall never look upon it without thinking of you, and I shall see it very often for it is on the table before me in my own room.

I think often, dear Mrs. ATWATER, if I outlive you, how much more I shall miss you out of the world than many with whom I have spent much more time on the earth.

I have not only long known you intimately through your life-long friend, Mrs. Baxter; but, in the realm of nature, you have seemed a close kin to me. I have a little California fern that you gave me long ago, and every time I look at it (and that is often), it seems to bind me anew to you. It is so fine, so perfect, so appealing—this most delicate expression of nature—and through all the vicissitudes of life the children of the natural world have been *so much to me*—no matter where or how life failed me otherwise—I have always found rest and peace under a tree. Your great love for nature, your fine perception, your keen appreciation of all her most exquisite forms, your love for this great tender mother of ours, has always made you dear among women to me.

And another trait in your nature has brought you even nearer—your wonderful sympathy for the dumb creatures of God, made to appeal so piteously, yet so often, in vain to the human kind. Your heart is large enough to hold all God's creatures—the dumb, the voiceless—so you see I have no uncertain reason for holding you dear upon the earth.

I am not so great a "philosopher" as you think. I meet calmly, as we all must, the inevitable. But to the final parting of dear friends, I never in my heart feel reconciled. It is so hard—even the promise of re-union does not quite comfort me. If I love my friend at all, I must love her as long as I exist in this life or in another. So no one dear dies to me. I sigh for her. I cry to *see* her; but, though I see her not, she ever abides with me as utterly as if I saw her always.

In your sickness, I sympathize as deeply with Mr. Atwater as with you. It must be as hard for him to *see you suffer*, as for you to suffer. My heart aches for him. As for you it seems as if I could not have it so. * * * *

Dear Mrs. ATWATER accept my tenderest sympathy and prayers, my life-long, loving memory. If not here, then hereafter *we shall meet again*, where there is no more parting nor dying, nor any more pain. With kindest regard to Mr. Atwater and the most sympathetic love for yourself.

Your friend,

MARY CLEMMER.

It is a long way back to the girlish letters, full of youth, hope, happiness and girlish affection, written in the wide bright rooms of the old Vermont homesteads.

Now these two women had planted, reaped and garnered their harvests. Life had brought to them both love and its fruitions. It had brought to them also loss. Death more than once had brought them desolation. One thing had outlived everything—unwavering, imperishable—their love for each other. It glows unworn, undimmed in their last letters to each other, as it did fifty years before in their first. Such a friendship not only sweetens life, it makes it larger and richer. Reaching on to "the Communion of Saints" within the vale, it strengthens one's faith in immortality. For the earth it makes us surer of womanhood by holding it inviolable in the high fine atmosphere of fidelity and unchangeable affection. A devotion between two women that never swerved through sixty years of mortal chance and change should be set high in honorable record.

In "Janette's" last letter to her friend, written but a few days before that friend's death, and just after she herself had been down to the very door of the Valley of Death, we find a spray of arbutus, just such an one as the girl might have gathered fifty years before out of the mossy coverts of the woods at Strafford, and one of the last acts of that friend's life was to place with her own hands into a beautiful box some of the daintiest treasures in her possession, including the rose-colored, strawberry-flecked neck-ribbon given to her by "Janette" nearly forty years before, now returned to its giver with other exquisite personal belongings. In a letter written by her to "Janette" from the Gardner House, Chicago, June 9, 1877, she says of this necktie:

What think you I saw when packing to leave 59I? The pretty little necktie—pink ground with white and red strawberries embroidered on it—your gift to me when married! just as bright and pretty as ever!

This box for her friend was discovered after her death, containing, in her own handwriting on a slip of paper, this inscription:

To My Dear Friend Janette, from Ella.

Mrs. Atwater wrote to Mrs. Baxter from Buffalo, November 27, 1877, the first detailed account of her disease. She said:

My Dear Friend Janette:

I have not been unmindful of your kind remembrances, the parcel of Vermont ferns and autumn leaves, and your kind letter received October 23d.

You are aware, through T.'s letter to the Doctor, that I have been very ill. He told him, doubtless, that two of our most responsible physicians, having made a thorough investigation, pronounce me a "very interesting case." Flattering—consoling—is it not? It is right that we endure physical suffering, I suppose, where science can be advanced.

* * * * * * * * * *

Honestly, Janette, I do not anticipate any permanent relief, and must summon even more than my wonted fortitude to endure to the end. My cough is more spasmodic than continuous. The effort of coughing increases the pain at the point of the right shoulder, which, at times, is so severe as to require sharp external applications for temporary relief. I can only rest in one position—on my left side—which, added to my other tribulations, renders the nights somewhat dubious. Six o'clock in the morning is my signal for leaving my wearisome couch.

4.

We had charming weather for our trip. Dr. C. forbid my leaving until we had experienced two days of sunny weather. They came at last. He said he should be thankful to have me deposited safely in Buffalo, for company counteracted all the good he might do for me. He positively denied company and conversation. (The idea—so beyond all precedent —of a woman holding her tongue.) Notwithstanding these injunctions, I received eighteen visitors on the day of our departure. Had not left my room in nearly three weeks when we were whirled into the depot. *   *   *   The old-time picture *en route* of gathering winter apples from prolific orchards was the first absolutely refreshing scene that had greeted me in many a day.   *   *   *   *   *   *   *   *

Among the last letters written at this time, was her last to her dear friend and teacher Mrs. Lincoln Phelps, of Baltimore. She writes, Christmas, 1877:

I cannot let the Christmas of 1877 and 1878 come and pass without giving expression to my unabated interest in and my deep-rooted affection for you.

You will perceive that I write from Buffalo. My physicians decided that hotel life was to exciting for me in my prostrate condition. We have therefore come to the home of my husband's niece for the winter. I am a recluse confined entirely to the house, and mostly to my room. My disease—solidification of the right lung, with other threatening symptoms of an alarming character.

She goes on to describe minutely to her friend the comforts and happiness of the home to which she had come— the home of her husband's niece, Mrs. Sexton, where a little more than four months later she entered into everlasting rest.

As the shadows deepened, and she drew step by step the nearer to the brink of the final river, we know how she felt by the last letter which she wrote to her friend " Janette " in Washington. She said:

BUFFALO, *January 30, 1878.*

MY DEAR JANETTE :

The old year has bid us farewell, and the new year is making rapid strides toward the same bourne—its termination, and you and I, physical sufferers, are mercifully spared. I know not how it is with you, but a continued earthly existence is with me hardly desirable. So long as you can *breathe,* Janette, do not murmur. My respiration is very laborious. The effect of walking across the room deprives me of the power of speech until I have a little recovered. My cough is exhausting and the pain in my shoulder terrific. Were they both continuous I could not long survive. Last night my shoulder was painted with morphine and iodine on retiring. Whether I have become more than ordinarily sensitive I cannot say, but I am frantic with the smarting until one o'clock. I have not been so affected in the other applications. So, Janette, if it is not one trial, it is another. Our physician, fortunately, is only three doors from us ; we were compelled to summon him a few nights since at two o'clock. He remained an hour with me. He is pronounced the best homeopathist in the city.

After detailing her symptoms, Drs. Cook and Johnson's diagnosis, she writes :

Were it not too late when the discoveries were made I should have gone straight to Washington to consult Dr. Jed. However, the parting time must come to us all, but it is sad to leave this beautiful world so at variance with it as all this physical torture renders one. I am confined wholly to my room—have been for three weeks. My rations are one-half a quail at a meal. On yesterday I sent down my entire breakfast untouched ; have no appetite, no rest. My good " T." is devotion itself, and will permit no one to do the slightest service for me. Only occasionally I receive a friend in my apartments, then with the injunction they do all the talking.

Now, Janette, I am only too happy to read from your letter that you can sleep, and converse, and eat. May God spare you yet a long time to your dear children and friends. I am willing and ready to obey His summons when it doth come ; still life is dear to me for the sake of loved friends. I have never been a society woman. My whole nature has revolted at it, but I have realized great enjoyment with nature, with dear friends, and in my pursuits. Let me hear just how you are when you are inclined to use the pen. I have not written of late, save when it was imperative. A letter has just come from the south of France, from our dear friends the Andersons ; say they will be here in June. I can hardly expect to greet them—possibly may.

Mr. Gooding is failing daily. Emma M. Taylor, of Havana, has recently sent me, from Cuba, a little box of curiosities. In her letter she deplores her father's condition. Did the holidays give you pleasure? They were sad to me. If elegant presents would make one joyous, I should have been so. I was only sorry I could not reciprocate as of old. I regret to learn through Maria of Mrs. Clemmer's sad accident. I shall make an effort to write her, inclosing my note to Maria, as I know not her address. I did not anticipate claiming so much of your time as a perusal of this long letter demands, but I have not written to you in so long a time.

I should be overjoyed to see the Doctor and his wife "in the spring," as you say, " *en route* " to California. If all is well with us I see not why this may not be possible. We have not, as yet, contemplated spring arrangements, there are so many dreary winter weeks to intervene. Strange as it may seem to you, we pine for Chicago and our Chicago friends.

When Mrs. Baxter received this letter her own life trembled in the balance. Months later it was given back to the many who love her, by a skillful surgical operation. After she had passed through this trial, which so easily might have ended in death, she, still feeble from suffering, wrote her last brief letter to the friend of her youth, sending it with the spray of arbutus, so full of youth and spring, into the chamber of decline and final triumph.

She writes :

March 9, 1878.

MY DEAREST E. :

Thanks for your kind and heartfelt congratulations. Yes! I passed through a severe ordeal successfully. The preliminaries were anything but pleasant. The success seems sure, but I assure you the fact that *you*, my dearest friend, are still suffering, detracts from my own rejoicing exceedingly. Your suffering is constantly in my thoughts, and I vainly wish some permanent relief could be discovered. You know I am with you in spirit as I would most surely be in flesh were it possible. * * I am still weak, but the wound is healing. God bless and comfort you both! Ever devotedly,

JANETTE.

I believe the last letter Mrs. ATWATER ever wrote, she wrote to her friend's daughter-in-law, Mrs. Florence Baxter, wife of Dr. J. H. Baxter, Chief Medical Purveyer, U. S. A., Washington, D. C.

176 FRANKLIN STREET, BUFFALO,
March 2, 1878.

DEAR MRS. BAXTER :

If it must be so—if dear Janette must pass through that terrible ordeal—thanks to you for so kindly and clearly conveying the intelligence. I was greatly shocked and grieved, as you can well imagine. The more I reflect upon the matter the more reconciled I become, especially as my physician assures me there is no fear of a return of the disease. He has performed a similar operation successfully—removing one breast—the lady at present being in perfect health. His only surprise being that the operation was so long deferred. Of what a burden are all your minds relieved. The promise of health to the dear invalid—dear to so many hearts—and the hope of her charming presence among you all for years to come must throw a roseate hue upon all your surroundings. God be praised for the attainments of science. Would that they might have fathomed my case. I will not speak of myself to-day. When Janette has recuperated a little, if I can guide my pen, we will hold converse. I responded to Mrs. Clemmer's kind note a few days since—this morning only have taken up my pen again. Thank you for your very kind letter.

My husband is writing to Mrs. Gooding, relative to Janette's condition. In the event of any unfavorable change, which is hardly to be thought of, pray let us be advised.

Mr. Atwater joins me in the most cordial love and congratulations to
dear Janette, the Doctor and yourself. Believe me, dear Mrs. Baxter,
Your warm friend,
ELIZABETH E. ATWATER.

The handwriting of this letter, written scarcely a month
before her death, shows in unwavering lines the same beautiful precision which was remarkable in her youth, and shows
with equal luster the unselfishness of her character, which,
amid the agony of her own dissolving nature, thought first
most tenderly of her friends, last of herself.

In great suffering, but with peace profound, she passed
into the final sleep and the forgetting.

Of those last hours that cloud this mortal life and opened
on the life everlasting, we find the touching account in the
words of Mr. Atwater. He writes to Mrs. Baxter from

BUFFALO, April 18, 1878.

MY VERY DEAR FRIEND:

Your very kind note of the fourteenth is at hand, and pray accept my
heartfelt thanks for it and its expressions of sympathy in my behalf.
From the relationship which has ever existed between yourself and my
poor departed wife, I can never cease to love you as her dearest, best
friend.

She suffered long and most intensely, and patiently. Begged her physician not to administer any medicine which would prolong her life. She
was ready, willing and anxious to depart and be freed from the constant
agony and suffering. She retained her consciousness up to about six
o'clock P. M. of the tenth, and from that time until she died (ten and one-
half o'clock A. M. of the eleventh) she was unconscious. She moaned
feebly during the night and until she ceased breathing, but died quietly
and without any violent struggle. * * * It was a dreadful sickness—
of terribly protracted agony. We all try to divest ourselves of selfishness, and to thank our Heavenly Father that He has taken her to himself,
and that she is relieved from suffering and agony.

My dear, good friend, such a wife as I have lost *ought not* to pass away from earth unnoticed and unannounced. Somebody should say *something* of her virtues, if she possessed any, and *you* know of and about her better than any other living being. I can *say* nothing. I may *know* much, but my tongue must be silent on that subject. Cannot *you*, my good friend, who have known her so long and loved her so well, give to Mrs. Mary Clemmer something of her history, of her attainments and characteristics, to enable her to give to the world some knowledge of a pure, good, devoted woman, of whom many have heretofore had no knowledge. It can do my poor dead wife no good, but it would be a great comfort and consolation to her many kind friends to know that, though dead, she was not forgotten.

My dear wife donated her entire cabinet of minerals and shells to the Chicago Academy of Science. To the Chicago Historical Society she gave everything relative to history. To the Old People's Home sundry gifts. To every one of her friends some memento. I find in a beautiful Tunbridge mosaic box sundry articles with a slip of paper in her own handwriting, "To my dear friend Janette, from Ella," which I shall forward to you soon. Very many of her rare and beautiful things are deposited in the Safety Deposit Vaults in Chicago, where they have been for three or more years, and I cannot distribute them until I return to Chicago, when the Doctor will hear from me.

She began the distribution of her effects three months before her death, but the work was very distasteful and unpleasant, and she often remarked that she was induced to do so to relieve me from so sad a task. She could do but little at a time and was unable to finish, but she gave me verbally her wishes, and I have endeavored to carry out her wishes in every respect. She selected all her own grave clothes three months before her death, and intimated to me fully her wishes as to her funeral and pall-bearers. * * * * Her nurse and physician became very much attached to her, she was so considerate and so patient. They both say that they never saw such suffering.

And yet to her last moment she never suffered so much that she did not think of others—often of others far distant—before she thought of herself.

Mr. Atwater's next letter is dated:

BUFFALO, *April 30, 1878.*

MY VERY DEAR FRIEND MRS. BAXTER:

Your kind note of the 22d instant was received as I was leaving for Canandaigua to make the necessary arrangements for interring the remains of my dear wife by the side of her mother in our family lot at that village.

I went there a week ago yesterday and caused a stone and brick vault to be constructed, under the direction of one of my old school-mates, a resident, and now about seventy-three years of age. I returned on Wednesday, and on Thursday my niece (Mrs. Sexton) moved into her new quarters. On Friday I received notice from my venerable friend that all was in readiness; when, with my nephew (Mr. Albert Barnard), of this city, I left with the remains of my dear wife for Canandaigua, where we arrived at half-past six o'clock P. M., and were met at the depot by my niece (Mrs. Brush, a sister of Mrs. Sexton's), several ladies, and ten of my old school-mates. The remains were taken direct to the cemetery, attended by the Presbyterian clergyman, and deposited in the vault prepared for them, by the side of her mother. It had rained hard nearly all day, but before we arrived at Canandaigua it became clear, bright and sunshiny, and it was beautiful. My old Canandaigua friends were exceedingly kind and attentive, and the few who had the pleasure of knowing her spoke of her with great kindness.

I remained at Canandaigua until three o'clock P. M. of Saturday, and reached Buffalo at eight P. M.; and I write you thus particularly because you were ever my dear wife's nearest and dearest friend, and would feel interested in knowing all about her.

Since her death I have been dreadfully lonesome and dreary, and have but little desire to do anything, see anybody, or go anywhere. She made very many bequests of trifles to her friends, and I have been engaged in hunting them up and sending them to the persons for whom they were designed. But she brought but few articles here, and I must finish up carrying out her wishes on my return to Chicago. You knew my dear wife well, but you would be astonished to find such method, such order, such detail. I find she has kept an accurate account of all her expenses ever since 1841—all written out in her books; and I find journals from

1860 up to *December, 1878*, written out fully every day, and giving a
complete history of each day of where she was, what she saw, and whom
she met in all her various travels to the South, through all the Southern
States and cities, to California, Colorado, etc., etc., with her views and
ideas of what she saw. These journals are interesting to me, as they take
me back over the same journeys, and bring everything fresh to my mind.
You have no idea of the world of work she has done with her pen.
Every letter she ever wrote or received is a matter of record as to the
persons to whom written, or from whom received, with the date thereof.
A full list of every person who called upon her, or upon whom she
called, I find extending back for years. I find memorandums in detail
of the contents of every trunk, box, bundle or package, and a full inventory of every shell, specimen, plant, shrub or curiosity ; where and how
she procured it, and in very many cases printed articles cut from papers,
giving a full history of the article or thing. I have had but little time to
examine her scores of books, filled full of memoranda, tied up and marked
by her. She has five thousand patriotic envelopes, designed to be placed
in books, and she has five large books (made for her in Philadelphia) in
which to place them, one of which is nearly completed, and the material
to fill the others ready. She has series of all the almanacs for this and
part of the last century, and an inventory of the number and of their dates.
Of her list of old spelling-books and of the books themselves I cannot
state accurately how many there are, but a great many. She has samples
of all the fractional currency issued by our government, and a world of
Confederate money, of all kinds and sorts and denominations ; as well as
a large assortment of individual or private *currency* issued by hotel-keep-
ers, merchants, butchers, etc., etc. I find that her cabinet specimens of
shells, minerals, etc., etc., are all numbered, and each box marked and
numbered, and an inventory made up of the contents of each box or
package, with the scientific name of each specimen. So with all of her
plants. Everything is in as complete condition as possible. The Historical Society will be enriched with a great number and variety of old
spelling-books and almanacs, and a variety of venerable literature. Was
a corresponding member of the Academy of Sciences of Maryland, and
also of the Academy of Sciences of Buffalo. Was one of the original
founders of the " Old Ladies' Home " of Chicago ; an active member of
the " Humane Society " of Chicago. She has always held a position as

one of the directoresses of the " Old Ladies' Home," and at one time was its treasurer. The Hon. George W. Clinton, an eminent botanist of this city, held her in high regard as a botanist, and says the very many specimens he received from her were prepared better than from any other person. She discovered several new plants, heretofore unknown in this country to botanists, and two or three have been named for her by botanists. My dear wife was a wonderful, wonderful woman, self-sacrificing, working always for others, and happy when she could in any way contribute to the happiness of others, at whatever cost to herself.

CHAPTER VII.

Tributes of Friends.

MANY personal tributes to his dear wife were received by Mr. Atwater. It would be pleasant to transcribe them all to these pages were it possible. As this cannot be, I give those which, springing from the most intimate knowledge, deal most largely and most minutely with her personal characteristics. First, the tribute to her dear memory from her life-long friend "Janette," Mrs. Portus Baxter, of Vermont. She says:

It is almost impossible to *specify* perfections in the character of my dearest friend ELIZABETH—her life from the beginning being faultless. Our acquaintance *with* and love *for* each other commenced when we were children, not more than six years of age, continuing, with constant correspondence, until her decease.

From childhood her innate sense of propriety was wonderful. Her devoted affection and large benevolence, controlled always by sound judgment and strict justice, gave weight and respect to her opinions. Small in stature, but in no other sense, she was full of animation and sprightliness ; gay, but never boisterous in her mirthfulness ; her wit and repartee sparkling, but never sarcastic. Her love of nature was intense, as her great knowledge *of* and interest *in* natural science testify. Botany was her favorite study in youthful and school-days, when we were intimately associated in study, always rooming together if possible. Her neatness and *order* were wonderful ; and my pleasure was unbounded when *our* room and our bureau drawers were pronounced "perfect !" Though *small* she was muscular, so much so we called her " Little Samson." That strength enabled her *small*, almost "petite" body, to accomplish wonders mentally and physically in the pursuit of every good work in which she engaged. There seemed no bounds to her endurance when interested in some benevolent or scientific object ; in truth, I have *never* known such an indefatigable, *earnest* worker in the various and praiseworthy directions suggested by her love of humanity or science.

Her love of animals was *very* strong. Once, in Chicago, when passing a teamster who had cruelly whipped his overburdened oxen, until the tough skin was broken and the blood starting, she very feelingly called his attention to it, asking how it happened. He was ashamed, and hung his head. She did not leave him without a promise he would not strike them again. She often saw horses and dogs abused, and never without a word in their behalf, so judiciously spoken they had the desired effect.

Many, many years ago, her father, Judge Emerson, induced the great revivalist Burchard to go to Windsor, where they resided, and make an effort to convert sinners. On asking the reverend gentleman concerning the prospect, he replied with earnestness : " Very well. I have strong hopes of your daughter ELIZABETH being converted." The father, with the utmost surprise, replied : " ELIZABETH ! ELIZABETH ! talk of converting *her!* Why, she is as pure as the angels in heaven !" Which announcement I conscientiously believe was true ; and no one had a better opportunity for *knowing*. Our intimacy from *childhood*, to the latest moment of her life, justifies the assertion that *human* nature can never attain greater perfection !

My admiration, respect and love for my dear deceased ELIZABETH can never be expressed in words, nor the sympathy and commiseration for her beloved and unutterably bereaved husband, whom it has always seemed to me was especially made for her. He was every way so compatible. In her last letter to me, January 30, 1878, she says : " My good ' T.' is devotion itself, and will permit no one to do the slightest service for me." Also (as we were at that time both invalids), after recounting her unfavorable and distressing symptoms, she says : " However, the parting time must come to us all ; but it is sad to leave this beautiful world so at variance with it as all this physical torture renders one. May God spare you yet a long time to your dear children and friends. I am ready to obey his summons when it doth come ; still life is dear to me for the sake of loved friends. I have realized great enjoyment with nature, with dear friends, and in my pursuits. I have never been a society woman; my whole nature has revolted at it."

Her heroism in her sickness and death was in unison with her rounded and perfectly Christian and consistent character, sustained through all her useful and eventful life. The last six months of suffering was *intense*, trying her patience and faith most severely, which was never found wanting. A true and earnest Christian, she has gone to the rest which God giveth his beloved.

The second tribute is from Mrs. Thomas Morris, a lady of marked intelligence and refinement, the wife of Mrs. ATWATER's nephew. Both husband and wife were great favorites and close companions of Mrs. ATWATER. Mrs. Morris writes:

POTOMAC, VA., *May 19, 1878.*
DEAR MRS. CLEMMER:

I have been looking over dear Aunt ELIZABETH's letters to-day, and find but one extract that seems to reveal the inner woman to the world. She says: "I must not write a word more. I have such distress for respiration, cannot cross the room without assistance. May God grant me submission to His holy will." This shows to us her unselfishness, her pen cheering us in this lonely place, though every stroke increased her suffering. She was truly a Christian in all her acts. Though you early heard her express in words her belief or hopes, she had not a particle of cant about her, and was the most natural, unaffected person I ever saw. With the nicest sense of propriety, she was the most girlish, playful creature among her intimate friends. That made her a companion you never tired of.

She was so sympathetic, she made warm friends among all classes of people; and she did not confine her sympathies to words, she was so generous. She was passionately fond of birds and animals, and often in the city stopped and pleaded for some dumb creature who was being ill-used. I well remember her once out paying visits, beautifully dressed, stopping and inquiring into the cause of a poor little mongrel dog's lameness, and stooping down in dust and dirt to look at the lame leg, the indifferent answer of the owner, and her indignation at the brutality of half the world.

She was order itself—did everything exquisitely. Her sewing was a marvel, and her pressed flowers the finest I've heard botanists say they ever saw ; and she had very valuable herbariums. Though she was in correspondence and constantly exchanging specimens with botanists in this country and Europe, I do not know what disposition she has made of these ; but intend going to Buffalo very soon to assist Mr. Atwater in looking over her effects, and can then write you ; and perhaps in settling quietly down with Uncle Sam. I may glean facts that will be of use to you ; if so, will write them down.

She was member of a number of scientific and historical societies, and has left many things to them, which I can tell you about by and by. Had a moss or fern named for her by some European botanist. She discovered it in California. She was never idle, and the number of letters she wrote was more than any one ought—so her physician often told her.

In her collection of rare things burned in the Chicago fire, she had contributions from every part of the globe nearly.

To illustrate how she made friends, and what grew out of the chance acquaintances : At the World's Fair in New York she was delighted particularly with the Italian department and the mosaics from Victor Emanuel s factory or pottery. She returned to look at them so often, and so thoroughly appreciated them, that she finally attracted the attention of the Italian Commissioner, a gentleman attached to the staff of the king, and they had many pleasant talks about art in general, exchanged cards, and within a year after his return to Italy came to her from him some exquisite specimens of the different kinds of mosaics and a photograph of Victor Emanuel, with his autograph. Since then, on the receipt of President Lincoln's photograph, she had from him a mosaic of the same, which is perfect as a likeness. Many pleasant letters passed between them, and a lasting friendship grew out of a chance meeting. So with a Nantucket sea-captain, whose wife she knew, but had never met him. Through a four-years' voyage he was constantly writing of this or that he had collected for Mrs. ATWATER—which finally reached her. She fairly inspired people thrown with her with her own tastes. She opened a new world to many by her genuine love for nature.

I shall never forget our rambles about Nantucket moors together one summer. She found Scotch heather there—just one tuft—a thing unheard of before in this country ; and then such a search for more, but in vain. The next summer I found it again in the same place, to her great joy, for some of her botanist friends had thought her mistaken, but another specimen convinced them, and she was credited with the discovery.

Her married life was as perfect as anything can be in this world. She was cherished and shielded from every care. I do not wonder poor Uncle Sam. sits down in utter desolation, for she did her share in making life sweet to him in a thousand womanly ways.

The following from Europe came from a correspondent of many years :

NICE, ITALY, *March 29, 1878.*

MY DEAR MR. ATWATER :

You will readily understand how much sorrow we have experienced from the contents of your letter of the 7th inst., which we received last evening. We entertained hopes that the wonderful energy and vitality which your wife's constitution had so many times evinced, might again come to her aid and yet preserve her to us all for yet a longer period ; but, from what you say as to her sufferings from pain and great weakness, I see not much hope of her long continuing in this life, and, my dear friend, why should we wish it, if so much pain and suffering is to be her lot ? for better happiness and absence from all sorrow in a better world, with a Blessed Saviour for her companion and where the weary are promised rest—by coming to Him. Blessed consolation for all who seek Him faithfully. May such be the inexpressible happiness of us all, my dear friend, when the hour of trial comes, for come it must to every one of us sooner or later.

This news throws quite a cloud over the prospect of our proposed visit to the West. To see our old and much-esteemed friend, your dear wife, once more, formed a large feature in our anticipated enjoyment in our trip, and now, I fear, such we are not destined to realize. Well, God's will be done, for in His keeping are we all. Let it be for us to strive earnestly to meet Him when He calls us away from this life, and to say with the German poet Neander, "I am ready, mighty Lord."

It must have been a very great source of thankfulness to you to be able to enjoy the comforts of so good a home for yourself and Mrs. ATWATER in this her hour of great trial, and that your own health was so improved as to admit of your constant watchfulness of her wants, and, I trust, without any return of your own past ailments. This must be a source of very great thankfulness to you hereafter, that you were enabled to be her constant companion. I know not if this may come to your hand that she may see it. I hope it may, and that you can read to her of all our grief and of all our sorrow to think we may not meet her again in this life. The many happy days—indeed I may say years—that we spent together at Chicago, and our constant happy intercourse since by correspondence, are things not to be easily forgotten, and we shall miss her wonted happy and most interesting letters *very, very* much. Many thanks for her kind thoughtfulness in sending us the pretty wild flowers. They will be treasures to keep and recall to our minds one of those happy features of her disposition—a love of nature—a most attractive souvenir of our very dear friend. I am writing this by candle-light, and I am very fearful you may not find it easy to read, for neither my sight nor my penmanship are so good as they used to be; but you must bear with my failings, for I am anxious that this may come quickly to your hand and go by to-morrow's post to Paris and, may be, catch the Cunard steamer on Sunday at Queenstown. And now, my dear friend, what more can I say, but that God may have you both in His keeping here and hereafter, and that such is my own and my wife's most earnest prayer. I seem as if under the influence of a dream in contemplation of this sad event, so pray excuse any blunders that may appear and be assured of our great love and esteem for both yourself and our dear friend, your wife. Tell her so if she yet be with you. Believe me now and always,

Yours faithfully,

P. ANDERSON.

The last is from a dear friend in Maine:

YORK HARBOR, MAINE, *August 20, 1878.*

MY DEAR FRIEND MR. ATWATER:

Your beautiful and most kind but truly sad letter, re-mailed to me from Cambridge, was duly received. I delayed answering it until I should know from Cambridge that the express package was safely received. A letter from Miss Lane's home assures us of its safe arrival. I thank you for the mementos and also for the tender recollections of our dear and faithful friend, your beloved wife. We thought we had known her methodical industry before your letter told us of it, but we had not conceived of its extent. Her patience in suffering, her active usefulness when health permitted, her untiring kindness, her consideration, her courtesy to all, her justice in all her dealings, we knew, and it is a terrible loss to us to feel that on earth we can know them no more. I am sorry that I did not know of your desire to have her friends' memories of her collected, with a brief sketch of her life in a memorial volume. It would have been a sweet, sad duty, and I should have felt I might in some poor way convey to her in heaven, and to you on earth, our appreciation of her, of your beautiful relation to each other, and of our gratitude for your long friendship. We were like sisters in those early Chicago days, and perhaps nearer to her than the friends made later after her life had broadened. I know her affection for "Janette," and I hope that if there were one thing more than any other that I should like to testify, it would be this: The fidelity and constancy of ELIZABETH'S nature. Though the circle of her acquaintance, and even of her dear friends, was constantly widening, yet she never slighted or neglected an old friend for a new. No one ever felt superseded and set aside. What she was in the beginning she was to the end, and if an old Chicago friend, after twenty years' absence from her, had met her in Jerusalem, she would have been welcomed so cordially that she would have been made to forget the lapse of years.

In this world of faithless friends and fickle fancies, I think this grand trait of our dear E.'s character should be held up to admiration and example. It would have been so easy for her, with her world-wide-apart friends, to have passed over and forgotten some ; but she never did ; and if she found a treasure in a new friend, she was ever eager to have all who had loved her before share it. I felt comforted to know that Katie Goodnow was with her to the last, she was so fond of her, and Katie was a true friend to her. I sincerely hope our good friend Will is not seriously injured. It would be a great blow to his sisters. I will not try to express to you the sympathy we feel for you. Always when I have thought of the happiest married pair, it has been of you two friends. You were always patient with her, devoted to her, and she knew it, and blessed

God for it. She was never tired of rehearsing your affectionate consideration for her, your patience with her invalidism, your indulgence of her tastes and anticipation of every wish. Her sufferings are ended. If we believe in a hereafter we can believe in nothing but good for her who tried to live honestly and deal justly with all. It is you whom we pity now. It is so *much* harder to be *left* than to be taken. We shed tears of sorrowful sympathy when we read of your sitting by her dying bed and helping her trembling hands to assort and arrange her last bequests to her friends. Indeed, sir, I do not see how you could endure the anguish of those last weeks; and I pray you may not be long parted. Miss Lane joins me in the most affectionate and grateful friendship and sympathy for you. From your old friend,

C. A. BAKER.

BUFFALO, *January 8, 1879.*

Madam: I am but one of the multitude who admired and esteemed ELIZABETH E. ATWATER. She has left her husband, my friend, in an enduring grief, which is, however, not the grief of those who are without hope. For myself, I deeply sympathize with him, and feel that I have lost a friend who was very dear to me.

Mrs. ATWATER's intellect was strong, her sense of beauty in all of its manifestations was admirable, her acquisitions of science great and diffused. Above all, she was in the truest sense a lady. Without effort, she commanded admiration, and won friends wherever she went. She was, to the utmost of her means, a promoter of science. She studied nature in a devotional spirit, and not as its cold self-seeking anatomist. I was more grieved than I can tell you at her departure, and I am glad that I have in the herbarium of our society so many and so precious memorials of her.

Very respectfully yours,

G. W. CLINTON.

Mrs. MARY CLEMMER.